C000231584

1 MONTH OF
FREE
READING

at
www.ForgottenBooks.com

By purchasing this book you are
eligible for one month membership to
ForgottenBooks.com, giving you
unlimited access to our entire
collection of over 1,000,000 titles via
our web site and mobile apps.

To claim your free month visit:
www.forgottenbooks.com/free164465

ISBN 978-1-5281-8925-5
PIBN 10164465

THE

REPORT

OF THE

ANNUAL EXAMINATION

OF THE

PUBLIC SCHOOLS

OF THE

CITY OF BOSTON.

1854.

BOSTON:
1854.
J. H. EASTBURN, CITY PRINTER.

CITY OF BOSTON.

In School Committee, February 24, 1854.

Messrs. Russell, Skinner, Norcross, Simpson, Sykes, Fuller, Haskins, Parks, and Drake, were appointed a Committee to make the Annual Examinations of all the Grammar Schools under the charge of this Board for the present year.

Attest: BARNARD CAPEN, *Secretary.*

In School Committee, November 7, 1854.

Voted, That the Committee on the Annual Examinations be authorized to report in print.

Attest: BARNARD CAPEN, *Secretary.*

In School Committee, November 14, 1854.

Dr. Russell, Chairman of the Committee to make the Annual Examinations, presented the Report of said Committee, which was accepted; and, thereupon, it was

Ordered, That the usual number—twelve thousand copies—be printed for distribution.

Attest: BARNARD CAPEN, *Secretary.*

REPORT.

In undertaking the task of the Annual Examination of the Public Schools, your Committee have felt that they had no light or inconsiderable duty to perform. The immense importance of the cause of education, and the large influence. which our common schools exert upon the public welfare have long been recognized in this community, and the responsibility resting upon those to whom the care of these institutions is committed, is fully appreciated by this Board.

The readiness with which the most liberal appropriations are made for the support of these schools, and the interest and pride taken in their success, are among the most encouraging signs of the times. It is undoubtedly true that, of all subjects that engage the public attention, no one has a more direct bearing upon the most important interests of the people, than the establishment and maintenance among them of good institutions for instruction. In this country, in particular, the theory of our government and the whole constitution of society demand, more than in any other, the most ample provisions for public education. And it is to the general recognition of this truth, and to the institutions that have sprung from it, that we owe, in a very great degree, whatever superiority we may possess as a community.

If it be allowed that, in facilities for the cultivation of the higher and more abstruse branches of learning, we are still inferior to other and older countries, that our universities and colleges cannot be compared with similar establishments abroad, which unquestionably afford vastly superior advantages to the small class of persons who can devote their lives to the pursuits of literature and science, we can claim, with truth, that we are surpassed by none in the number and excellence of those institutions which have for their object to cultivate the general intelligence and to diffuse useful knowledge among all classes of the people. It is our superiority in these respects which is the conservative element of our society, securing us from the dangers to which our form of government might expose us, and giving us confidence in the strength and stability of our social organization.

The City of Boston has for a long time enjoyed a high reputation for the excellence of her public schools. We believe this reputation to. be, on the whole, well deserved. Our schools are, in general, well conducted, under the charge of able and accomplished teachers, and their interests are carefully watched over by the city government. Most of the changes which have been made, from year to year, by this Board, have been attended with beneficial results.

New and improved school houses have been erected; by the abolishing of some schools and the enlargement of others greater facilities of classification have been obtained; more care has been exercised in the selection of masters and assistants; and by the recent increase in the rate of compensation for teachers, better opportunities are afforded for obtaining the services of the best qualified persons. These and other improvements, recommended by experience, and introduced after careful consideration, have done much to raise the standard of instruction in our schools, and to render them worthy of the continued confidence and support of the community.

It is not to be supposed, however, that our school system has attained the perfection at which we should aim, and it does not become us to boast of our success or to rest satisfied with what we have already accomplished, while there are still many deficiencies to be supplied, many errors to be corrected, and many improvements to be made, before we can be entitled to say that we have done our whole duty towards our schools. The increasing wants and demands of the times require the exercise of unceasing vigilance and care in the management of these institutions. Some of the deficiencies to which we allude may be easily corrected. Of others it must be left to time and a more enlarged experience to discover and apply the remedy.

It is only by slow degrees that the true methods for the advancement of any art or science are perfected. Many steps in the wrong direction must be retraced, many false theories exploded, and many imperfect systems overthrown before the truth is finally discovered. The science of education is no exception to the general rule. The principles which should direct it, though plain and simple when once perceived, have been with difficulty recognized, and some of the most important of them are, as yet, perhaps, but imperfectly understood, or if understood not practically applied.

The great principles are even now too frequently overlooked, that every true system of education must, as far as possible, correspond with and assist in the natural course of the development of the mental faculties, and that the cultivation of the intellect and all the higher powers of the mind must be an intelligent process. Our methods are apt to be too mechanical, and not sufficiently addressed to the understanding and the reasoning powers of the learner. They proceed too often upon the ground that the pupil is a machine, from which a certain amount of work is to be expected, rather than a being endowed with reason and intelligence, to be carefully trained and educated according to the laws of his nature. On this account his progress becomes tedious and difficult, and he loses the benefit to be derived from the high enjoyment which is the natural attendant upon intellectual activity, when directed to its appropriate channels.

To the young, the first steps in the acquisition of knowledge and the exercise of the intellectual powers are evidently attended with the greatest satisfaction and delight. It too often happens, however, that those occupations which should continue to give intense pleasure, become in the school room a mere drudgery and a task. It must be owing to some great error in our views and practice on this subject, that such a perversion of the natural instincts should have become almost the rule rather than the exception.

If it were possible to introduce into all our schools the correct methods of education, so that the various elements of knowledge might be presented to the mind of the pupil in their true and natural order, and with due regard to their adaptation to the development of his faculties, the actual amount of knowledge acquired, as well as the beneficial effects of the process of acquisition upon the intellect and character, would be greatly augmented. A new interest in their pursuits would be awakened among the pupils, their understanding of the principles of the subjects studied would be facilitated, the memory quickened, the faculty of attention strengthened, and the general powers of thought called into action. A keen and vivid enjoyment would take the place of that listless inactivity of mind which is too often observed, and which is, of all others, the most discouraging and hopeless hindrance to intellectual progress.

That an approach to this state of things is possible, is evident from the success which has attended the efforts of those teachers who have best appreciated these principles. They have known how to make study attractive as well as profitable to their pupils, so that the hours devoted to school are looked forward to with pleasure, and employed with satisfaction and advantage. Education, with them, implies something more than the mere study of books, the mechanical performance of certain tasks, and the committing of pages to memory. It extends to the cultivation of all the powers of the intellect, the improvement of the taste, the guidance of the imagination, and the elevation and refinement of the whole character.

EXAMINATION.

The Annual Examination was held during the two weeks preceding the vacation at the end of May. It has been usually deferred to the latter part of June or July, at which time the schools are preparing for the annual exhibitions and for the medal examinations. In order not to interfere with these preparations, and to avoid the excessive heat of the summer months, it was thought best this year, to examine the schools at an earlier period. This arrangement was found more convenient than the usual course, both to teachers and pupils, and it had also the advantage of enabling the Committee to observe the schools in their usual condition, and as they are ordinarily conducted, without any special previous preparation for examination.

The examination was as thorough as the time allowed to each school would permit, and though it was not possible to examine "all the classes in all the studies," as prescribed by the Regulations, it is believed that the Committee have been able to form a sufficiently accurate estimate of the comparative merits of the schools, and of their general condition.

Every school was examined by as many of the members of the Annual Examining Committee as could conveniently attend, with the aid, in most instances, of some other members of the Board, and of the Superintendent of Schools. A critical examination was made by the Chairman, of the first class in each school, in all the more important studies, and every room in each school was visited by him personally, and its condition observed.

Your Committee have endeavored to conduct the examination in such a way as to obtain a knowledge, not merely of the amount of instruction actually imparted to the pupils, but, what is of far more consequence, of the methods of teaching adopted, the kind of mental and moral discipline employed, and the general influence exerted by the teachers in each school.

The subjects proposed embraced all the studies prescribed by the Regulations, from spelling, reading and the first operations in arithmetic, to those requiring a higher degree of cultivation and more maturity of thought. The first classes, as well as the younger, besides the usual examination in the higher studies, were carefully examined also in the elementary branches, your Committee considering it a well established principle that a thorough and accurate acquaintance with these is an essential requisite to a good education. It has been supposed by some, that an attention to the higher studies is apt to lead to neglect of the elementary branches. This, however, is not found to be the case in our schools. On the contrary, it has been almost universally observed, that those teachers who have best known how to educate the minds of their pupils to the successful pursuit of the higher branches of study, have, at the same time, best understood the importance of accurate instruction in the earlier studies, and an intelligent acquaintance with the first principles of knowledge.

On the whole, your Committee find much reason for encouragement in the result of the examination, and they believe that the condition of the schools will compare favorably with that of previous years. We have fewer inferior or indifferent schools; some of those which were formerly deficient have improved; while our best schools continue to maintain a high rank, and to afford means of education such as are enjoyed, probably, at few institutions of a similar kind in the country. The general good discipline in these schools, the amount and accuracy of the instruction given, the interest manifested by the pupils, and the high qualifications of the teachers, are among the most gratifying evidences of the success of our system of public instruction.

It is satisfactory to observe that these advantages are more and more appreciated by the community, and that many of the more intelligent class of parents, some of whom have heretofore hesitated to send their children to the public schools, are beginning to avail themselves of the opportunities offered in them.

It is on all accounts desirable that those whose home advantages and education would enable them to exert a salutary influence on their fellow pupils, should attend the public schools, while the wholesome experience which such schools afford, will not be without its value to themselves, in promoting a spirit of self-reliance, and enlarging their acquaintance with the actual world.

The vigilance with which these schools are watched over by the community, and the careful supervision exercised by this Board, make it unlikely that any great abuses, if such should occur, should long continue to exist in them, and if cause of complaint is at any time found by any citizen, the remedy is at hand in an appeal to the Sub-Committees, who are always ready and anxious to examine into and remove all just grounds of dissatisfaction.

In regard to the character of the instruction given at the public schools, experience, we believe, has fully demonstrated, that pupils educated in them are at least as thoroughly instructed, in all the more important elementary branches of study, as those taught in the best private schools.

We have referred to certain schools as inferior to others in point of merit, and we are reluctantly obliged to admit that, notwithstanding all the care and attention bestowed upon our schools, we have still some which fall below the standard which might be attained, and the excellence which we have a right to expect and demand. The inequality of merit in our different schools, and even in different classes of the same school, is a matter of daily observation, and it is important that its causes should be understood. If we could discover the reasons why some of our schools have attained to a high degree of excellence, while others are deficient in many important particulars, we might perhaps be able to remedy some of the defects of the latter, and to raise the standard of all.

The varying material of which the different schools are composed, and the unequal home advantages enjoyed by the pupils, are no doubt among the causes of the inequality referred to. The greater conveniences, and superior advantages for classification and arrangement, of some school buildings, may also have an influence. But, in the last result, it will be found that it is the ability, industry and fidelity of the teachers, which, more than all other causes combined, determine the character of a school.

That this is the case is evident from a comparison of schools having equal advantages in all other respects, as well as by comparing the different classes, in those schools where each teacher has a separate room. In some rooms we find good order, industry, a love of study, and a marked proficiency in the pupils, which are not observed in the departments under the care of other instructors. It is upon the master chiefly that the responsibility of the government and direction of a school must rest. His influence should pervade every department, and the success or failure of the whole depends in a great degree upon his character and qualifications. The master, however, must depend much on the efficient aid and co-operation of his assistant teachers, and in the selection of these, as well as in every other arrangement of the school, his responsibility is shared by the Sub-Committees, and through them by every member of this Board.

Since the character of the schools is so intimately dependent upon that of the teachers, it is evident that the selection and appointment of suitable instructors is the most important office of this Board, and one to which all its other duties are subordinate. It should be especially careful to employ those teachers, and those only, who by their interest in the pursuit, their thorough education and their general fitness for the duties of the station, show themselves worthy to be entrusted with the charge of our schools.

In the selection both of masters and assistants, no

other motive should influence the members of this Board, than the desire to obtain the services of the best qualified persons. Motives of personal feeling or kindness towards individuals, should never, in any case, be brought into competition with our regard for the highest interests of the schools. It is a mistaken philanthropy to allow teachers to remain in the service, who, from loss of interest in the profession, the neglect of it for other pursuits or business, or from any other causes, have become disqualified for the proper performance of their duties. The removal of an incompetent teacher affects one individual only, but the evil consequences of retaining such an one in the schools fall upon a large number of persons, and the injury done is irreparable. We would, however, advocate a proper liberality towards those teachers who, after long and faithful public service, are compelled by sickness or infirmity to retire from our schools. They deserve our respect and gratitude, and we shall be held responsible by the community, in whose name we act, for a just and considerate course of conduct towards them.

The selection of the large number of teachers required for the wants of this City, is a duty demanding the exercise of much judgment and discretion, and it is possible that some changes might be made in the manner of their appointment, which would secure a greater degree of certainty in the result. Some means should be devised by which the Board may be enabled to become more fully acquainted with the character and qualifications of all the various instructors, than they can be under the present system. The nomination of subordinate teachers may safely be left in the hands of the Sub-Committees, subject to the confirmation of the Board. But the annual election of masters, the most important duty which we are called upon to perform, too often takes place without sufficient previous deliberation and consultation, and without adequate opportunities being afforded to members, of forming a correct opinion in regard to the merits of candidates. It is evident to your Committee that some change is needed in our regulations and in our practice in this respect, but the particular methods by which the desired result is to be obtained, they would leave to be determined by the future action of this Board.

The importance of employing able and efficient assistant teachers is not perhaps sufficiently recognized. Their influence begins at a time when the minds of the pupils are•most susceptible of bias, and continues long enough to make a deep and permanent impression upon the character. The large number of assistants now required in our schools, makes it often a matter of difficulty to obtain such as are competent to fill the vacancies which are constantly occurring. Your Committee take pleasure in referring to the success of the City Normal School in supplying this want, and they would recommend to those masters and Sub-Committees who are in need of teachers as substitutes, or to fill vacancies, to take advantage of the opportunities which it offers. It will be seen by the report of the Sub-Committee of that School, that a considerable number of its pupils have already been appointed to permanent places as teachers, and it is not too much to say that those who have received such appointments, have approved themselves to be at least as competent and efficient as any assistants employed in our schools. Some of them have been promoted, after a short probation, to the post of Head Assistant, with the full approbation and consent of the masters and Sub-Committees of their respective schools.

In these suggestions your Committee would not be understood as intending to imply any want of confidence in our present able corps of instructors. They are industrious and faithful public servants, laboring patiently, day after day, in a vocation which more than any other is destined to affect the well being of the community. They deserve to be sustained and encouraged in all their efforts to improve the character and increase the usefulness of the schools under their charge. The large proportion of them, we are confident, appreciate the responsibility of their position, and apply themselves cheerfully and conscientiously to the performance of its duties.

There are, perhaps, a few among them who need to be reminded of the important nature of their profession, and of the necessity of devoting themselves to it with renewed life and energy. They allow themselves to fall into a habit of looking upon their occupation as a mere routine in which they take but little interest, and which they regard as only an interruption of their other pursuits. They forget that a good instructor has always something to learn as well as to teach. Every teacher must be also a student. He must keep his own mind and intellect alive and active, if he would excite the interest and enthusiasm of his pupils.

Perhaps the inequalities above noticed, in the different schools, may be traced to the different course pursued by teachers in this respect, more than to any other cause. Those who regard their duties as limited to the mere routine of the school room, and requiring but little habitual exertion on their part, and no continued effort at self-improvement, soon lose their own interest in their pursuit, and fail to produce any beneficial influence on their pupils. Other teachers are constantly aiming to improve themselves as well as

their pupils by reading and study on subjects connected with the daily lessons, as well as on others of a
more general character, and by a sincere and zealous
effort to do every thing in their power to promote the
interests of their schools. The good effect of their
exertions is at once apparent in the increased intelligence and mental activity of their pupils. No teacher
can keep himself fully prepared for his duties without
much study and thought, as well as a true and sincere
interest in his work.

The studies pursued even at our Grammar Schools,
cover so large a ground, that the labor of years would
be insufficient for a full acquaintance with all that is
to be known in regard to them, and the branches
connected with them. We do not, indeed, expect
that the pupils will acquire more than the first rudi-
ments of some of these, but in order to understand
them thoroughly himself, and to be able to explain
their principles, it is necessary that the instructor
should be far in advance of his pupils, and able to
take a comprehensive view of each subject studied,
as a whole, as well as in its details.

The masters of our schools have an important and
arduous duty to perform, and one involving a large
amount of responsibility. The duties of the assistant
teachers are equally important in their place, and demand the same degree of interest in their work, and of
careful preparation for it, if they would maintain their
rank in the estimation of those to whom the charge
of the schools is committed. It must be, at the same
time, an encouragement and a stimulus to both masters
and assistants to reflect that the progress of their
pupils is watched with anxiety by many parents and
friends,—that the whole community is interested in

the result of their labors, and is ready to award to them the full measure of respect and consideration which is sure to follow a conscientious and successful performance of duty.

TEXT-BOOKS.—Next perhaps in importance to the subject of the appointment of teachers, is the selection of suitable text-books for the use of the pupils. It is true that good teachers will produce good results even with inferior means, and that no teacher ought to be dependent upon the text-books, but it is no less true that well-written and thorough text-books are almost essential to complete success in teaching. The various explanations and suggestions from the teacher, required even with the use of the best manuals, necessarily occupy much of his time, and he cannot afford to have so large a portion of it expended, as too often happens, in supplying the deficiencies of inadequate books.

Your Committee would suggest that more care is necessary than has hitherto been taken, to exclude unsuitable books, and to secure the introduction of those only of the best character in each branch of study. It has too often happened that books of at least very doubtful merit have been introduced into our schools, by the perhaps well intentioned efforts of authors and publishers, without a sufficient examination. Instances have occurred in the history of this Board, of the adoption of books, without due consideration of the consequences of precipitate action on this subject.

No book ought to be adopted without a thorough examination of its merits, and a favorable report by an appropriate Committee. It is desirable and proper that such Committee should, if they see fit, consult with experienced teachers in regard to any book brought to their notice ; but the custom, which appears to be gaining ground, of allowing authors and publishers to offer to the Board the signatures of the masters, in favor of their own publications, obtained for the purpose of superceding other books already in the schools, is one which ought not to be encouraged.

In regard to the text-books at present in use in the schools, your Committee believe that some improvements might be made, and they would recommend the subject to the particular attention of the Board.

We have some books in daily use which, if they had been more carefully examined, would never have been introduced into the schools, and others which ought to be superceded by better books on the same subject, which have been since published. We would not, however, recommend any extensive and sudden changes without due deliberation, and the certainty that the change proposed would be an improvement.

Without dwelling too much on the details of this subject, we may refer to the text-books in reading and arithmetic as particularly requiring notice.

The reading books for the higher classes have the merits of good judgment and taste in the selections, and they are perhaps equal to any that have been prepared for the purpose. All of those used by the younger classes, however, cannot be spoken of in the same terms of praise, and some of them are quite unworthy of a place in our schools. Some of these contain pieces which are beyond the reach of the understanding of the pupils by whom they are intended to be read, with others which are trivial both in style and matter, and in some instances, not written with due regard to the rules of grammatical construction.

A good reading book for any class should contain selections from the best writers in the language, prepared with a reference to the cultivation of the taste, and the education of the intellect, at the same time that they serve as exercises in reading. It requires the same judgment and discrimination to compile books for the younger pupils as for those of a more advanced age. Our language has many classical authors, of correct taste, and pure and simple style, selections from whose writings would be quite appropriate for the youngest classes, as well as for older pupils.

The extent of the influence of the reading books upon the character of the pupils, is not, perhaps, sufficiently considered. With some, whose opportunities for reading at home are limited, they are the chief means of their acquaintance with the best writers of our language. There are many who owe their first impressions of beauty in composition to these books; and there are probably few who have ever learned to read at all, who do not, in after life, remember and recur with pleasure to the selections of prose and poetry from the masterpieces of our literature, which have been rendered familiar to them through their class books at school.

The text-books of arithmetic, also, need a careful revision. Our regulations now allow the use of seven different books on arithmetic. Some of these are probably unnecessary, and might be dispensed with; others are not well adapted to the wants of the pupils, from their deficiency in a full and complete analysis of the principles of the subject. There are many excellent recent works on arithmetic, which teach, not by rules to be committed to memory, but by a thorough explanation of methods and principles. If any of these are found to be superior to the books now in use, the interest of the pupils requires that a change should be made.

The text-books in other branches should also be carefully examined, but we are not prepared to recommend any definite changes in them at the present time.

DISCIPLINE. Your Committee have been happy to observe an improvement over former years in the general character of the discipline of the schools. The moral influence of the instructor appears to be gradually superceding the harsher methods of discipline, and teachers are beginning to discover that appeals to the higher motives of action, even in the younger classes, are the most efficient means of securing obedience, industry and a love of study.

It is to be regretted, however, that these views are not more generally adopted by all teachers in our schools. It appears, upon investigation, that some of the severer methods of discipline are still employed, and that even corporal punishment, which, in the opinion of your Committee, should be had recourse to only in rare and exceptional cases, is practised in some schools to a greater extent than they conceive to be necessary or expedient. Corporal punishment is permitted by our Regulations, and we would not take the power of inflicting it out of the hands of the masters, because there are, or may be, cases of aggravated misconduct which only this form of discipline can reach. But that it should be a matter of daily occurrence in any school, and inflicted for slight and trivial causes, we regard as a just ground of reproach, and as an evil which ought to be remedied.

We are aware that this mode of punishment is defended by some persons as the only efficient means of influencing refractory pupils. It is not to be denied that order is the first law of the school room, and that obedience and submission to the authority of the teacher must be maintained and asserted at almost any sacrifice. Cases may occur of direct insubordination where other means have failed to produce submission, and where the infliction even of severe punishment, may be necessary and salutary. Such instances, however, must be rare in every well regulated school and we cannot but regard the frequent resort to this means of asserting authority, by any teacher, as evidence of want of the ability to command respect by force of character and moral influence.

Though temporary submission may be obtained by physical force, the state of mind which follows it is not generally favorable to future amendment. The immediate advantage gained by corporal punishment is, in most cases, more than counterbalanced by its permanent ill effects both upon the teacher and the pupils who receive it, as well as on those who are only spectators. The constant habit of witnessing it, must have a demoralizing effect upon any school. There is also great danger that, where it is resorted to on every occasion of misconduct, it may sometimes be inflicted unjustly by the teacher, in a moment of excitement, or adopted as the readiest means of enforcing order, where milder measures would have been equally successful and less objectionable.

Your Committee have learned, with surprise, that corporal punishment frequently occurs in the rooms of some of the assistant teachers. The elevating and refining influence of female teachers, has usually been referred to as a reason for employing them, to a large extent, in our schools. It was hoped that this influence would render unnecessary a frequent recourse to appeals to the sense of fear. Such is found to be the case in many instances, and our best teachers have least need of a resort to corporal punishment in the government of their classes. A power of this grave nature should, in any case, be committed only to those who know how to use it with judgment and discretion, and, as a restraint upon its too frequent exercise, your Committee would recommend that all the provisions of the Regulations, chapter 1st, section 10th, be carefully insisted upon by the Sub-Committees.

In most other respects the general discipline of the schools is highly commendable. Much progress has been made, of late years, in the cultivation of a right tone of feeling and a kindly intercourse between the instructors and their pupils, which is promotive of mutual confidence and respect. Where this state of feeling exists in the highest degree, it supercedes, to a great extent, the necessity for the usual methods of discipline. A love of study for itself, and for the advantages which it brings with it, and a generous desire to secure the approbation of their instructors, and to promote the interests of the school, are found a sufficient stimulus to the pupils, without the need of other rewards or punishments.

It has occurred to us, however, that in a few of the schools the principle of emulation is somewhat too freely resorted to as a motive for exertion. It is not possible entirely to exclude this principle from a school, nor, perhaps, is it desirable to do so. But a too frequent appeal to it is so liable to overstimulate the ambition of pupils, and to excite unpleasant and envious feelings in their minds, that we should wish to see it very seldom employed. A laudable desire to make the greatest possible attainments in study, and to improve every advantage offered, should be approved of and encouraged, but it should never be allowed to degenerate into a mere personal ambition to excel, from a love of distinction or for the sake of reward. No apparent temporary advantage ought for a moment to be compared with the injury done to the moral sentiment by an appeal to an unworthy motive, or by anything tending to interrupt the harmony and good feeling which should always prevail among the fellow-pupils in a school.

The system of gradations of rank, according to marks for good or bad scholarship and deportment, which has been long employed in our schools, is useful to a certain extent, but it is in many respects objectionable, particularly in those schools where the pupils are led to attach too much importance to the distinctions created by it. There are graver objections, however, to the system of awarding medals in the manner at present adopted, and the advantages thought to be derived from them are, in the opinion of your Committee, very questionable.

The possession of these medals is acknowledged to be a very uncertain test of merit. From five to ten pupils out of each school are annually selected to receive this distinction, and the difficulty and almost impossibility of making a just award in all cases, must have been felt by every Sub-Committee who has had this duty to perform. The merits and claims of candidates are often so nearly balanced that a very slight and hardly appreciable difference may turn the scale, and the decision sometimes causes a feeling of disappointment on the one side, and of imaginary superiority on the other, equally without just foundation in either case.

It must also frequently occur, that among the disappointed candidates at one school are some who are quite as fairly entitled to the distinction as those who have received it at another school, where the number of competitors happened to be smaller, or the standard of attainment not so high.

Other objections to the awarding of medals might be mentioned, but your Committee have thought it proper to offer only the above observations on this subject, and to suggest the expediency of some modification, if not an entire abandonment, of the present system.

The beneficial tendency of the Annual Exhibitions, as conducted in many of our schools, has been seriously questioned by some of our most experienced teachers. They have complained of the loss of time and the interruption to the regular course of study, caused by the usual preparations for these occasions, and have remarked upon the false impressions which they give of the comparative merits of the schools. It is, on all accounts, desirable that the parents and friends of the pupils should have opportunities to observe the progress and conduct of the schools, and the Exhibitions might be conducted in such a way as to obtain this result, and, at the same time, serve as a healthy and beneficial stimulus to the pupils. They should aim to show, not what display a class may make after weeks of careful training and drilling for a special occasion, but the real progress they have actually made in their studies, the amount of useful information they have gained, and the whole result of the methods of instruction and government employed, and of the influence exercised over them by the teacher. Nothing should be done for mere effect, or to exhibit a superficial brilliancy in the place of solid attainments.

In this connection we would mention, with commendation, the special care taken by some masters that each individual in a class should receive his just share of attention and assistance in his studies. There is a tendency in certain schools, perhaps fostered by our system of Exhibitions, to put forward the brightest scholars, and to bestow an undue share of time upon them, while those of inferior capacity or less attainment are comparatively neglected. The injustice and impolicy of this course are evident. Every pupil has an equal right, according to his industry and application to his duty, to receive the full benefit of all the means of instruction provided by the city, and no personal feeling of partiality, or the gratification of the natural desire to exhibit a brilliant class, should lead a teacher to favor any portion of his school at the expense of the rest. It is, besides, undoubtedly true that the most prominent pupils at school are not always those who, in after life, become the most valued and respected members of society. The mind and character are developed according to laws which are beyond our scrutiny, and our calculations are constantly liable to error. It is not precocious brilliancy of intellect, but those moral qualities which lead the scholar to perform all his duties faithfully and to improve the time, which will determine his future position.

We also observe with satisfaction the arrangements made for the accommodation of those pupils whose circumstances will not permit them to attend school during the whole of the year. These are often deserving and intelligent scholars, who are desirous of taking advantage of all the means of education which they can obtain, during the time which they are able to devote to this object. They should be cordially received into our schools, and suitable provision should be made for them, either in separate classes or otherwise, as may be found most expedient.

. Representations have been sometimes made by parents to the Board, that the pupils, particularly at the girls' schools, have been overtasked, and that an excessive amount of study has been required by some teachers. That there may have been some foundation for this complaint, in a few instances, is probably true, but your Committee cannot find that the evil complained of has existed to any great extent, and they have reason to believe that it has been remedied in those schools where it did exist. It is fully understood by the teachers that study, however important, should never be allowed to interfere with health. Nothing is to be gained by overtasking the pupil, but, on the contrary, irreparable injury may be occasioned by it. Even if physical health does not suffer by too much study, the mind may be impaired by the large demands made upon it, by too close attention to a great variety of subjects.

The time of the school hours should be fully and profitably employed, but the most ample opportunities for healthful exercise, and for a large amount of salutary recreation out of school, should also be allowed. But a small amount of actual study out of school, should be required, even of the oldest pupils. To the younger classes none but the shortest and simplest lessons, if any, should be assigned to be learned at home.

Much depends upon the manner in which instruction is given, and upon the state of mind of the student. He should be encouraged to look upon study as a source of enjoyment rather than as a task; but, to be fully enjoyed, requiring the highest exertion of his faculties, and a thorough interest in his work. What is taught should be clearly and definitely explained, so that when once learned it is fully understood and not easily forgotten. A few things intelligently studied will make more impression and be of more permanent benefit than a much larger amount hastily and carelessly passed over, and one hour spent upon any lesson when the mind of the pupil is active and interested in the subject, is better than many hours passed in listless poring over books. The pupil is not then constantly obliged to retrace his steps to study over again what he has at first but imperfectly comprehended.

The actual amount of knowledge obtained at school is not so important as the habits of thought and methods of study acquired. The time, however, spent in the school course is fully sufficient, if well employed, for the acquisition of a large amount of instruction, and all that is necessary or important to be learned up to the age at which our pupils leave the Grammar Schools, might be easily attained without any excessive amount of study.

In addition to the objections, on the score of health, to the practice of assigning too many lessons to be studied out of school, another evil is that these lessons occupy the time which ought to be at the disposal of pupils for the cultivation of the mind by general reading. One of the deficiencies most observed among pupils, even of the older classes, in our Grammar Schools, is the want of that general cultivation which only an intelligent course of reading can give. Their attention is so much confined to their text-books and to their peculiar school studies that they do not find time for general reading, or if they have time, they are not sufficiently encouraged and directed how to improve it. Pupils will frequently give an excellent recitation on some subject, for example, of ancient or modern history, while they are quite uninformed in regard to the great events that are passing in the world around them. Some exercises of a more general character might well be introduced among the more common school studies, which should lead the thoughts of the pupil to a more extended view of the relations of these to other branches of knowledge. His reading out of school might be so directed by his instructors, as to promote a general acquaintance with literature and science, and at the same time to improve his taste and enlarge the range of his thoughts.

The use of the Public Library, so freely extended to the pupils of our schools, may be of great advantage towards this object, if properly understood. There is perhaps no class in the community to whom the Library may be made more directly beneficial than to these pupils, if the selection of books to be read by them is made with discretion and judgment.

It should, notwithstanding, be considered, that however important the education of books and of school may be, these are only subsidiary to the wider education which comes from the experience of every day life, and that the great end of the whole should be to prepare the student most thoroughly for the duties and responsibilities incident to his future position.

Your Committee have not thought it advisable to give comparative tables of the results of the examination in each school, but they propose to arrange the observations suggested by it in regard to each branch of study, under its appropriate head.

SPELLING. Much attention has been paid to obtain accuracy in spelling, in many of the schools, and in some of them with very good results. We have still, however, to notice some deficiencies in this branch. The average number of errors, in a list of words in ordinary use, selected for the purpose of examination of the first classes, was far greater than was anticipated, and shows the necessity of an increased attention to this subject. It would appear that the ordinary drilling from a spelling book or dictionary, though highly useful, is not sufficient of itself, to insure even a creditable degree of accuracy. Many errors were committed by classes who had been frequently and carefully taught in this way. Various expedients are practised in the different schools, with more or less success, to aid in obtaining a more favorable result. In addition to these, we would suggest that each pupil be required to keep a book in which to write all the words given out at each lesson, to study carefully those mis-spelt, and to be prepared in them at the succeeding lesson. The pupils should also prepare lists of words, selected by themselves, as they occur in their reading or study, to be given out by them to the class, and each pupil should take his turn in this exercise. The words should be both written, and spelt orally by the class. Other expedients may be suggested by the ingenuity of the teachers or of the pupils themselves, to excite an interest in the subject, and it is very desirable that every means should be tried to ensure the greatest possible degree of accuracy in this essential part of education.

READING. The proficiency of pupils in reading is perhaps one of the best tests of their general intelligence and mental development. Much attention was therefore given to the examination in this branch. The same diversity of merit in this respect as in most others, is found in the different schools, depending perhaps mainly on the taste and ability of the teachers. In some schools an intelligent and expressive manner of reading is cultivated, in which, without any effort at theatrical display or forced and unnatural emphasis, the sentiment and meaning of the author is given with a truth and simplicity that leaves little to be desired. In other schools a style of reading has been introduced and encouraged, whose object would seem to be to leave truth and nature out of view, and substitute an artificial standard in their place. This system aims to teach what emphases and cadences are proper to express any particular emotion, and to apply them to the piece to be read, instead of making the pupil first understand what he reads, and allowing the emotion or sentiment itself to suggest its own manner of expression.

The artificial habit of reading, acquired in this way, is one of the worst faults into which a pupil can fall, and it is unfortunately too prevalent in our schools. It would be easier to teach a pupil who had never learned to read at all, than to correct the bad habits which this system has sometimes produced. We believe the elocutionary rules so much insisted upon in our books, to be partly the occasion of this fault. They are, in our opinion, not only useless but positively injurious. When a pupil understands what he is reading, such rules are superfluous, and if he does not understand, no rules can help him. It is well for a pupil to know the vocabulary of the subject, that he may be able to express himself definitely and intelligibly in regard to it, but it is a mistake to suppose that a familiarity with all the technical rules of dramatic elocution is necessary to make a good reader. We need a more intelligent and less mechanical method of teaching, which shall accustom the pupil to express the thoughts of another, in reading, with the same ease and facility that he expresses his own thoughts in speaking. There seems to be no sufficient reason why all should not be able to do this, if the proper methods were adopted from the commencement of their course of instruction.

WRITING. Your Committee have observed, with pleasure, a good degree of proficiency in writing in most of the schools, and an increased attention to the subject in all. Some of the specimens exhibited at the examination were remarkable for their beautiful and finished execution. It would perhaps be better, however, if more of the time devoted to writing were spent upon what is essential and practical, rather than upon the ornamental branches of the art. It should be the aim of the pupil to acquire a fair, distinct and plain hand-writing, rather than to attempt what is called elegant penmanship. In this point of view some of the systems now in use are decidedly objectionable, and we are sorry to see them taking the place of the old methods, by which the pupil was taught to form the single letters carefully and correctly, before proceeding to the practice of running-hand. The results obtained by the old method, when faithfully pursued, of learning to write from copies in a large round hand, without superfluous ornament or display, were more satisfactory, in most respects, than those of the later systems. The unnatural and ungraceful attitude at the desk while writing, which has been lately introduced into some schools, must also lead to inconvenient habits, which it will be difficult for a pupil to correct after leaving school.

The change made last year in the Regulations, allowing the Sub-Committees to introduce such systems of penmanship as may be found most expedient in their respective schools, will probably be beneficial. No one system can be well adapted for all pupils, and any system which requires a uniform method of writing from all, must fail of being the most useful to the larger proportion of them. The hand-writing of each individual must be peculiar and characteristic, and it is not desirable, even if it were possible, to make all write according to one uniform plan. We have known a class of pupils in one of our best schools whose hand-writing, previously good, and in some cases excellent, because plain, distinct, and having individual character, was, in our opinion, seriously injured, and reduced almost to a uniform mediocrity, by a series of lessons from a professed penman.

GRAMMAR. Notwithstanding the inherent difficulties of the subject, the pupils generally, and those of the higher classes in particular, appear to be well instructed in this branch of study. Many of the exercises in parsing and in the analysis of sentences showed much intelligence and correct habits of thought. A tendency may be observed, however, in some schools to look upon grammar as a science having no relation to our ordinary speech, and not applicable to our daily communication with each other. Some pupils, who could parse and analyze remarkably well, used incorrect language in conversation ; and frequent inaccuracies of expression were observed even in the discussion itself of the rules of grammatical construction.

Grammar is simply an abstract of the fundamental laws and principles of language, and English Grammar is the expression of those laws as applied to our own tongue. All instruction, therefore, on the subject, to be practicably available, should be such as will lead the pupil to form correct habits of expression in his own use of language, in conversation and writing. This is a point which needs to be insisted upon, because it is frequently overlooked. The errors and mistakes constantly made by pupils, are too apt to pass without correction by the teachers, and it must even be confessed that all of the teachers themselves are not sufficiently careful in their own use of language. It should be remembered that in this matter, more perhaps than in any other, practice is better than precept, and no teaching of grammatical rules will counteract the injurious effect of the frequent hearing and use of ungrammatical language.

In view of the fact that bad habits of speech when early acquired are extremely difficult to eradicate in after life, it is advisable that the study of grammar, in some form, should be very early begun in the schools. The instruction in the first years should be chiefly oral, and of the most practical kind. Any errors that may be committed should be carefully corrected, and the habit of accuracy early and firmly fixed. The higher departments of grammar should be entered upon at a later period, when the mind is more mature, and the careful and critical study of this subject in all its relations, will be found one of the most interesting and useful pursuits in which students can engage.

ARITHMETIC. This study is one of those in which much accurate and careful instruction is given in our schools. In some of them the practical part of the subject is very thoroughly taught, and the pupils show a remarkable degree of facility and correctness in the solution of even difficult and complicated problems.

Sufficient care, however, is not always taken to make the pupil understand the principles of arithmetic, and the reason for the processes performed. We have frequently, for example, been pleased with the facility with which a class have solved problems involving complicated operations in fractions or in proportion, but on inquiry for an explanation of the reason for the various steps of the process, no answer could be given, except that such was the rule of the text-book. No attempt seemed to have been made to analyze these rules, and to investigate the principles upon which they are constructed. This fault may be partly owing to deficiencies in the text-books themselves, in regard to analysis, but it must also be attributed partly to want of sufficient care on the part of the teachers to draw the attention of the pupil to this subject. Pupils seem sometimes to imagine that the rules of the text-book are arbitrary directions given by the author of the book, rather than applications of the general laws of the relations of numbers to particular classes of cases. No scholar can be considered as well instructed in arithmetic unless he can arrive at the solution of the problem before him independently of any given rules. A thorough analysis of one question will enable him to construct rules for himself applicable to the whole class of similar cases. The unnecessary multiplication of rules, however, is in itself an evil, and it is better that every problem should be considered and solved on its own merits. By this method of studying arithmetic, the mind of the pupil is kept awake, and his intellect excited, and, while his progress is facilitated, the subject itself is better understood, and he obtains all the advantage which the study is capable of affording, as a mental exercise.

The beautiful simplicity of the principles of arithmetic, and the wide extent of their application, can hardly fail to be appreciated, and to excite an interest in the minds of all intelligent students, when the subject is presented to them in a proper light.

The advantage of oral and mental arithmetic, as it is at present pursued, is very apparent. The introduction of that class of books on arithmetic of which Colburn's was among the first, and is perhaps still, in many respects, the best, has been of great benefit in promoting the intelligent study of the subject. The importance of written arithmetic, however, should not be overlooked. Exercises on the slate or the blackboard should accompany every lesson, and even the youngest pupils should be taught to explain, with the pencil, all the processes which they have mentally performed. We make this observation because it is frequently found that pupils, who are confined too exclusively to mental arithmetic are apt to commit errors, when called upon to perform even the more common and simple operations, on the slate.

While recommending a more thorough analysis of the principles of arithmetic, we would, at the same time, urge the importance of a greater exactness in the performance of the earlier processes. The result of the Examination shows that mistakes in simple numeration, addition, subtraction, multiplication and division are among those most frequently made, even by advanced pupils. Much of the time occupied in the solution of the more complicated problems would be saved to the pupil by a greater facility and habitual exactness in performing the common operations. If the pupils in the younger classes were more thoroughly taught the importance of habits of correctness, at the very beginning of the study, mistakes of this kind would less frequently occur.

Much advantage would also be gained by an early and careful analysis of the steps of these simpler processes. The difficulties, for example, which invest the subject of decimals, in the minds of some pupils, might, it is believed, be wholly removed by a clear understanding of the principles of numeration, while a definite comprehension of the whole subject of the addition, subtraction, multiplication and division of fractions would easily follow upon a full explanation of these operations as applied to whole numbers.

GEOGRAPHY. Much attention is paid to geography in our schools, and generally with a good degree of success. It is one of the most interesting studies to the pupils, and one of the most profitable of the course, when properly pursued. Too much time, however, may be given to minute details, and to the attempt to remember the situation of comparatively unimportant places on the map, in such a way as to confuse the mind of the learner and divert his attention from those broad features which form the groundwork of the science. Much unprofitable labor is sometimes spent upon these minor points, and we believe it to be a fact, that a very large proportion of all the knowledge of this kind acquired by the pupil, is forgotten immediately on his leaving school, unless circumstances occur to bring it into daily use.

The general outlines of geography should be first studied, with the use of the globe and such other apparatus and diagrams as are necessary to fix the chief points definitely in the mind. The main features of physical geography come next in importance; such as the outlines of continents and oceans, the situation and direction of mountain ranges and great rivers, and the principal laws which affect climate and temperature. Political geography should be connected with the preceding, in the natural order. A definite acquaintance with its grand divisions should first be formed to serve, as a skeleton or groundwork for future acquisitions. The outlines of the chief divisions of the globe, the extent, resources and government of the various countries, the situation and history of important places are then more easily fixed in the memory.

The propriety of connecting the study of geography with that of history is here apparent. Political geography changes with every great epoch of history, and its boundary lines are the landmarks of states as they rise and fall. Its condition at any particular time is a summary and result of the history of the world to that period.

If we compare the map of the world as the ancients represented it, with that drawn by Columbus, or with the delineations of our own time, we shall hardly recognize any resemblance. The outlines of the political divisions of North America at the period of the landing at Plymouth, or of the revolution of 1776, were as different from each other as those of both periods are from the divisions of our day. A series of drawings representing the boundaries of the countries of Europe at the different stages of its political progress, would be a most instructive illustration of history.

HISTORY. It is not to be expected that great acquisitions should be made in history during the years of the school course. The knowledge, however, which is acquired should be of that definite and practical character which will form a well grounded foundation for future advancement. We have heard recitations in this branch from some pupils with very great pleasure, and the intelligent answers often given to general questions on the subject have shown a good degree of proficiency. The interest of pupils in the study would probably be increased by not confining them too closely to any text-book, but by taking up special points or periods of history in succession, and encouraging the pupils to seek additional information in regard to them, from all sources within their reach, till they had acquired a sufficient familiarity with the subject to appreciate the true way in which all history should be studied.

COMPOSITION. Some of the exercises in English Composition have been very gratifying to your Committee, showing a maturity of thought and facility of expression which was hardly to be expected from pupils of the age of those in our Grammar Schools. In no exercise is the intelligence of a pupil so thoroughly tested as in this branch. It would be well if more attention were paid to this subject in all our schools. The habit of composition might be begun at a very early period. There would appear to be no reason, in the nature of the case, why it should be more difficult to express our thoughts on paper, than in common conversation. It is probable that much of the difficulty often complained of in regard to composition, arises from the want of the early cultivation of the habit of writing. If pupils were early required and encouraged to express their own thoughts, in a familiar way, in writing, to make abstracts of what has interested them in books or lectures, or to give written accounts of what they have seen or heard, they might acquire a much greater facility in composition, than they at present possess. We would not intimate the opinion that by this course all could become elegant writers, but we believe that it is possible to make a large proportion of pupils able to write their own language at least correctly and intelligibly.

In those schools where elocution is frequently practised, a facility in speaking is acquired, even by those not naturally disposed to it. We would encourage, in every way, the cultivation of the faculty of expression of thought, whether by writing or speaking, and we should be pleased to see a greater variety of exercises, adapted to this end, introduced into the schools.

DRAWING is one of the exercises required by our Regulations, but no special system has been adopted, and no means for regular instruction in it provided. It has been left to accident, or to the ability and taste of the teacher to decide how much, if any, attention shall be given to it in each school. Some very excellent specimens have been exhibited at the examinations, and such an amount of skill evinced as to show that, with proper encouragement, drawing might become a very important and useful auxiliary in the schools. The cultivation of the eye and hand by drawing has been heretofore too much neglected. We should be glad to see the practice of illustration by the pencil, or upon the blackboard, much more extensively introduced into the schools, and made familiar both to the teachers and pupils, and we would recommend that some definite provision be made for the purpose of instruction in this important branch. This might probably best be done by the appointment of assistants in each school, with special reference to their ability to teach in this branch.

PHYSIOLOGY. This subject has been studied with much care in some of the schools, but it does not appear to have been attended to, in all of them, in the most judicious manner. Too many pages of the text-books are taken up with anatomical details, and the attention is not sufficiently directed to the general laws of health and their application. It is desirable that all should be acquainted with the most important and interesting points in the structure of the human frame, but your Committee doubt the expediency of allowing anatomy to occupy so large a part as it now does, of the books of physiology used in our schools. We need a text-book which shall, in a few simple pages, set forth all that is necessary to be taught to pupils on the laws of health and the rules for its preservation, and it should be considered the duty of teachers, so far as their influence goes, to see that these rules are not only known but practically applied.

In NATURAL PHILOSOPHY, ALGEBRA, GEOMETRY, and other permitted but not required studies, the proficiency is various, according to the attention paid to these subjects. In some schools they are not studied at all, while in others a good degree of familiarity with some of the most important of them has been attained.

While we would not advocate attention to these at the expense of the other and essential branches of study, we are of opinion that something more might be done in the higher studies than is now aecomplished. Pupils who remain in our schools till the age of sixteen or seventeen, and some of whom have been, several years in the first classes, ought to be well instructed in some of the more advanced studies, besides having a thorough knowledge of the elementary branches. If the time spent in learning the latter were employed in such a manner that these should be early and thoroughly mastered, a portion of the labor, now expended in going over nearly the same ground from year to year, might be profitably employed in making still further progress.

SEWING. The introduction of Sewing into the younger classes of the schools for girls, during the last year, has been attended, so far as your Committee have been able to learn, with very satisfactory results. It is the general testimony of the teachers that the experiment promises to be a very successful one. The sewing does not interfere with the progress of the pupils in their studies, but forms an agreeable and interesting relaxation, as well as a useful occupation, in the intervals of study. It is found to be also an additional advantage to a large class of pupils, in promoting regular attendance at school. The benefit derived by them from the instruction given is recognized by all who have examined the subject.

Your Committee have now made all the observations which have occurred to them, during the Examination, in reference to the merits and defects of the schools, and have suggested such improvements as they have thought might be of utility. They have not hesitated to express their opinions freely, knowing that these institutions, so well conducted, and so highly appreciated, are able to stand the test of criticism, and cannot be injured by any remark having for its object to improve their condition. If they have pointed out plainly some of the defects which seem to them yet to exist in our school system, and to interfere with its efficient working in particular cases, it is with a sincere desire to aid in remedying those defects, and to make our schools still more worthy of the high reputation which they already justly enjoy.

LE BARON RUSSELL,
OTIS A. SKINNER,
LORING NORCROSS,
DANIEL P. SIMPSON,
JAMES N. SYKES,
ARTHUR B. FULLER,
J. PROCTOR HASKINS,
LUTHER PARKS, Jr.,
HENRY A. DRAKE.

GRAMMAR SCHOOLS.

Abstract of the Semi-Annual Returns. *July*, 1854.

SCHOOLS.	Boys.	Girls.	Total.	Average attendance last six months.	Seats.	Between 5 and 15.	Over 15.	Masters.	Sub-Masters.	Ushers.	Female As'ts.
Latin, - -	171	-	171	156	210	107	64		1	3	0
Eng. High,	146	-	146	* 149	225	30	116		2	2	0
Normal, - -	-	140	140	137	150	-	140		0	0	4
Model, - -	86	-	86	88	116	86			0	0	2
Bigelow, - -	-	364	364	326	448	345		9	0	0	8
Bowdoin, -	-	559	559	592	560	503			0	0	10
Boylston, -	414	287	701	696	774	691			1	1	10
Brimmer, -	541	-	541	547	558	528			1	1	8
Chapman, -	262	261	523	498	563	496			0	0	11
Dwight, - -	384	280	664	614	670	629			1	0	10
Eliot, - - -	604		604	631	696	593			1	1	11
Franklin, -	-	594	594	573	800	571			0	0	11
Hancock, -	-	636	636	625	672	615			1	0	11
Hawes, - -	393	-	393	348	360	386			1	1	4
Johnson, - -	-	324	324	275	355	303		2 1	0	0	5
Lyman, -	304	327	631	558	726	619			1	0	10
Mather, - -	311	316	627	575	560	610			1	0	11
Mayhew, -	462	-	462	426	600	455			1	1	8
Phillips, - -	451	-	451	456	540	443			1	1	7
Quincy, - -	616	-	616	647	732	604	1		1	2	9
Smith, - -	32	58	90	54	80	83			0	0	1
Wells, - - -	-	481	481	399	488	460		2 2	0	1	6
Winthrop, -	-	400	400	352	444	372			0	0	8
Totals.	5,177	5,027	10,204	9,722	11,327	9,529	675	26	14	14	165

* These returns are made in July, when the number belonging to the Schools is small ; hence the *average attendance* for six months is in some instances greater than the number belonging to the School at the time of making the return.

LATIN SCHOOL.

The Annual Examination of the Latin Grammar School was made on the fourteenth and fifteenth days of July; and the results of it were satisfactory to the members of the committee, by whom it was conducted.

The present condition of the School justifies the high reputation, which it has long enjoyed in our community.

The regulations require that candidates for admission shall be ten years of age, and shall produce certificates of good moral character from the masters of the schools, which they last attended.

The great accession of numbers to the school since the change, made two years since, in regard to the age of admission, seems to afford evidence that that change has met the approbation of the citizens.

The increased attention to the branches of a good *English* education, which this change and the longer term allotted to a regular course through the school, justify, without detracting from the thoroughness with which the branches, peculiar to this school, are cultivated, will undoubtedly lead parents to present their children at the early age, which the present regulations permit ; in order that they may have the advantage of the complete course, without postponing their entrance into college to too late a day.

Candidates for admission are examined in reading, writing, spelling, arithmetic, geography and grammar.

The regular course of instruction continues for six years, but pupils may be advanced, according to scholarship, so as to complete it in a shorter time. Instruction is given in the several branches required for admission, and in declamation, English composition, history, ancient geography, algebra, geometry, drawing, and in the French, Latin and Greek languages.

The dead languages are taught with uncommon thoroughness.

The number of pupils is at present two hundred and three; and they are under the care of one master, one sub-master and three ushers. The state of the school proves the faithfulness of the teachers.

The building occupied by it in Bedford street is well adapted to its purposes, and is in good order.

It is believed that no institution of the kind offers greater advantages to those, who propose to themselves a collegiate education.

At the annual visitation of the school, the Franklin medals were awarded to Joshua G. Beals, Wm. P. G. Bartlett, Henry L. Patten, Samuel H. Eells, Thomas Reed and William Everett.

For the Committee.

J. THOS. STEVENSON.

ENGLISH HIGH SCHOOL.

The Sub-Committee of the English High School respectfully report that they attended to the Quarterly and Annual Examination of said school, on Tuesday, the 18th of July; three members of the Committee being present.

The general condition of the school was in all respects satisfactory; and the examination of the graduating class, to which special attention was paid, gave conclusive evidence of thorough and faithful instruction, of diligent improvement of privilege and opportunity, and of good preparation for the various departments of active life, upon which the members of this class were about to enter. It may be recollected that in their annual report of last year, the Sub-Committee, without proposing any specific change in the course of study, suggested that perhaps the English High School had become too exclusively scientific, and that more attention should be given to the English language, its literature and history. During the past year, Mr. Sherwin, without neglecting the prescribed studies, has sought to remedy this defect, by oral instruction, lectures, and the use of such books as the limited Library of the school affords; so that at the visitation of the school on the 18th ult., the Committee were surprised and gratified to find that the first class, after a thorough examination in Natural Theology, Moral Philosophy, Christian Evidences, Astronomy, Natural Philosophy, and the French Language, were also able to give a good general outline of English Literature, and to mention the names, works, characteristics, and some events in the lives of many of the prominent English writers from the time of Spencer and Shakspeare to the present day. The Committee regard the action and efforts of Mr. Sherwin in this respect, as in the right direction, and with the instrumentality of a good Library of standard English authors, which will soon be placed in the school, the Committee trust that he will be enabled to raise this department of English literature to a level with the scientific and philosophical departments, and to give the pupils under his charge a large and generous culture in the history and literature of their own language.

In this connection, the Committee regard with much interest an event which occurred during the past year, viz: the formation of an Association of the Alumni of the English High School. There are various ways, direct and indirect, in which such an association may exert an influence favorable to the best interests of the school. By a letter from the President of this Association, Frederic U. Tracy, Esq., the Committee are informed that a considerable sum of money has been raised by subscription, which it is proposed to appropriate in such ways as may be deemed best to the benefit of the school; and in the first instance, the Association offers to make the beginning, to lay the foundation, of a good Library of standard English authors and works on History, provided the City will furnish cases for the accommodation and preservation of the books, in one of the rooms of the school. As this request is reasonable, and one that in other similar instances, this Board has been ready to meet, the Committee append to their report an order to this effect.

From the same source, also,—the President of the Association,—the Sub-Committee learn that a gentleman, willing and competent, has been agreed upon to make the selection of mineralogical specimens, offered to the High School, by Francis Alger, Esq., from his rich and valuable cabinet; so that we may hope that the school will open the next year, with a valuable collection of minerals, and a small, it may be, but well selected Library of English Classics, in addition to its present instrumentalities of culture. Something will also be done, in due time, by the Association, towards embellishing the rooms of the school, so that they shall wear an aspect more gratifying to the eye than at present, and tend to refine and elevate the tastes and awaken pleasant thoughts and emotions in the minds of all who have to pass six and seven hours of every day within them.

The Philosophical Apparatus of the school is well appointed, in good condition, and has been much used during the year, in giving instruction in the various departments of Natural Philosophy.

These are the favorable aspects in the condition and prospects of the English High School.

There are other aspects and events, less favorable, which the Sub-Committee must bring to the consideration of the Board. The first is the resignation by Mr. Francis S. Williams, of his office of second sub-master of the school. His long connection with the school as usher and sub-master, his talent and tact as an instructor, the persevering self-culture by which he has made himself a thoroughly accomplished scholar and teacher, and the influence exerted over his pupils by his high character and amiable manners and deportment, all conspire to make Mr. Williams' resignation a great loss to the school. It is matter for congratulation, however, that his large experience and eminent qualifications as a teacher are not to be lost to the general cause of education; and while we regret that his services are no longer to be rendered in the English High School, the length and fidelity of his past labors in this School, demand that our best wishes for his success attend him in the new sphere of private enterprise and instruction upon which he is about to enter. The Committee hope to nominate as his successor, one, who if not at once equal to him, will by perseverance and fidelity ultimately make his place good.

Another unfavorable point to which the Committee would briefly allude, touches the relations between the English High and the Grammar Schools.

According to the plan or the theory of our system of public instruction, it ought to be an object of ambition in each of the Grammar Schools to furnish the largest number of pupils, thoroughly prepared, for the English High School; and the success and usefulness of the Grammar Schools should be tested in a great measure by this result. Whatever these schools can teach above and beyond this, in studies not required for admission to the English High—because more thoroughly taught there—let it be taught, and if other things are not neglected, let the teaching be commended; but the test of the school—at least one of the chief tests—should be the number of pupils in whom a desire is awakened to pass on to the English High School, and who are found to be thoroughly grounded and qualified in the studies required for admission to that school.

This is the theory of our school system. Such however is not the result of the practical working of the system. The number that come to the High School from the Grammar Schools is not so great as it ought to be; and those who do come are not so well prepared as they ought to be. At the recent examination, eighty-five candidates presented themselves for examination, of whom fifty-four were admitted; the other thirty-one will have to undergo a second examination with new candidates at the close of the vacation. When the whole examination is completed, the Sub-Committee will make the report upon the subject which the Regulations require.

Without going into a discussion of the causes of the difficulty, and of the imperfect relation, practically, which the English High and Grammar Schools sustain towards each other, the Committee would suggest that perhaps something might be done to remedy the difficulty by adopting a different mode of admission into the English High School. It might be made the duty of the Annual Examining Committee to attend to this matter. In their annual visitation of the Grammar Schools, they should determine by examination, how many of the pupils of the first, or first and second classes are qualified to enter the English High School the next September, and their certificate to that effect should secure their admission; the master and Sub-Committee of the English High School having reserved to them the power, at the end of the first term, or at the Thanksgiving vacation, to discharge from the school those whom it was found, after three months' trial, were not able to go forward with the course of instruction and study appointed for the school. Or the certificate of the master of a Grammar School, endorsed by the Chairman of the Sub-Committee of his school, might be taken as prima facia evidence of qualification, and the pupil received upon that—with the same provision as in the former case—that if not found able at the end of two or three months to go on usefully with the course of studies at the English High School, the master and Sub-Committee be authorized to dismiss him.

The Sub-Committee do not propose any specific plan or order for this change. They simply throw out the suggestions for the consideration of this Board at some future time, or for the consideration of those who may come after them in office. The English High School is not the least important part of our great system of public instruction. By our merchants, master mechanics, architects, civil engineers, in all the higher departments of active life among us, the pupils of this school are eagerly sought for, and readily obtain good situations.

The poorest boy in the City, thoroughly educated at the English High School, is sure to attain to an honorable and useful situation in life.

Nothing should be done, therefore, to injure this school, or diminish its advantages or its influence; but every effort should be made to increase and diffuse its advantages, and to bring the largest number possible to partake of them.

Respectfully submitted.

S. K. LOTHROP.

Ordered, That the Sub-Committee be authorized to procure Book-cases, for the use of the English High School—at an expense not exceeding Three Hundred Dollars.

NORMAL SCHOOL.

The Sub-Committee of the Normal School respectfully report,

That the Annual Examination of this school was held in July. It is now two years since the school was established, and the first class of pupils have accomplished the course of study originally proposed. The present condition of the school is highly satisfactory, and the success of the plan adopted has been such as to show the importance and utility of this institution as a part of our system of instruction.

Frequent applications have been made at the school for pupils to act as teachers in other schools. Many of them have been engaged as substitutes, in the Grammar Schools, for teachers temporarily absent, and more than twenty pupils have received appointments to permanent places as teachers. The reports of the Sub-Committees and masters of those schools in which they have been employed, give evidence of the very gratifying success which has attended the efforts of these pupils in teaching. There are other pupils remaining in the school who are as thoroughly qualified to teach as those who have left it, but, with the permission of the Board, the Sub-Committee have allowed such members of the senior class as desired it, to continue in the school for another year, as an advanced class. These pupils, besides attending to their own studies, will be prepared to fill any vacancies which may occur in the other Schools.

The course of study pursued has been nearly such as was at first proposed, with, however, a liberal construction of the regulations which allow the introduction of some of the higher studies, in addition to those usually taught in the Grammar Schools. Among those introduced have been Algebra, Geometry, Physical Geography, Rhetoric, Moral and Intellectual Philosophy, English Literature, with a critical analysis of classical writers, and the study of the French language. It will be observed that the list of studies successfully pursued at this school, differs but little from those of the best High Schools for Girls. The methods of pursuing these studies, however, have been carefully adapted to the chief objects of a Normal School, and much effort has been made to enable the pupil to acquire so thorough and complete a knowledge of the subjects studied, as to qualify her to teach and explain them clearly to others.

The Model School continues to be of much use in affording opportunities for observation and practice to the pupils of the Normal School, and the instruction given to its pupils is at least equal to that of the other Grammar Schools. Some inconvenience, however, has arisen from the small number of pupils which the Model School will accommodate, and the limited field for practice which it affords. If arrangements were made by which our best Grammar Schools should offer such opportunities as are needed by those who are preparing to become teachers, the present Model School might be dispensed with. A cordial co-operation of the masters of the Grammar Schools with the instructors of the Normal School, in giving their valuable advice and assistance to such pupils as should be sent, from time to time, to those schools, to observe, and learn the best methods of teaching, would be of very great advantage towards the accomplishment of the end proposed.

The Annual Examination of candidates for admission to the Normal School, took place on the 27th o July. The whole number of candidates was sixty three, of whom fifty-two were admitted. Thirteen can didates presented themselves for examination at the commencement of the school in September, of whom nine were admitted.

The whole number of pupils at present in the school is as follows :—

In the advanced Class,	-	-	-	31
In the Senior Class,	-	-	-	61
In the Junior Class,	-	-	-	61
				——
Total,	-	-	-	153

The number of pupils in the Model School, is 103.

For the Sub-Committee.

LE BARON RUSSELL, *Chairman.*

CPSIA information can be obtained
at www.ICGtesting.com
Printed in the USA
BVHW081906231118
533755BV00012B/243/P